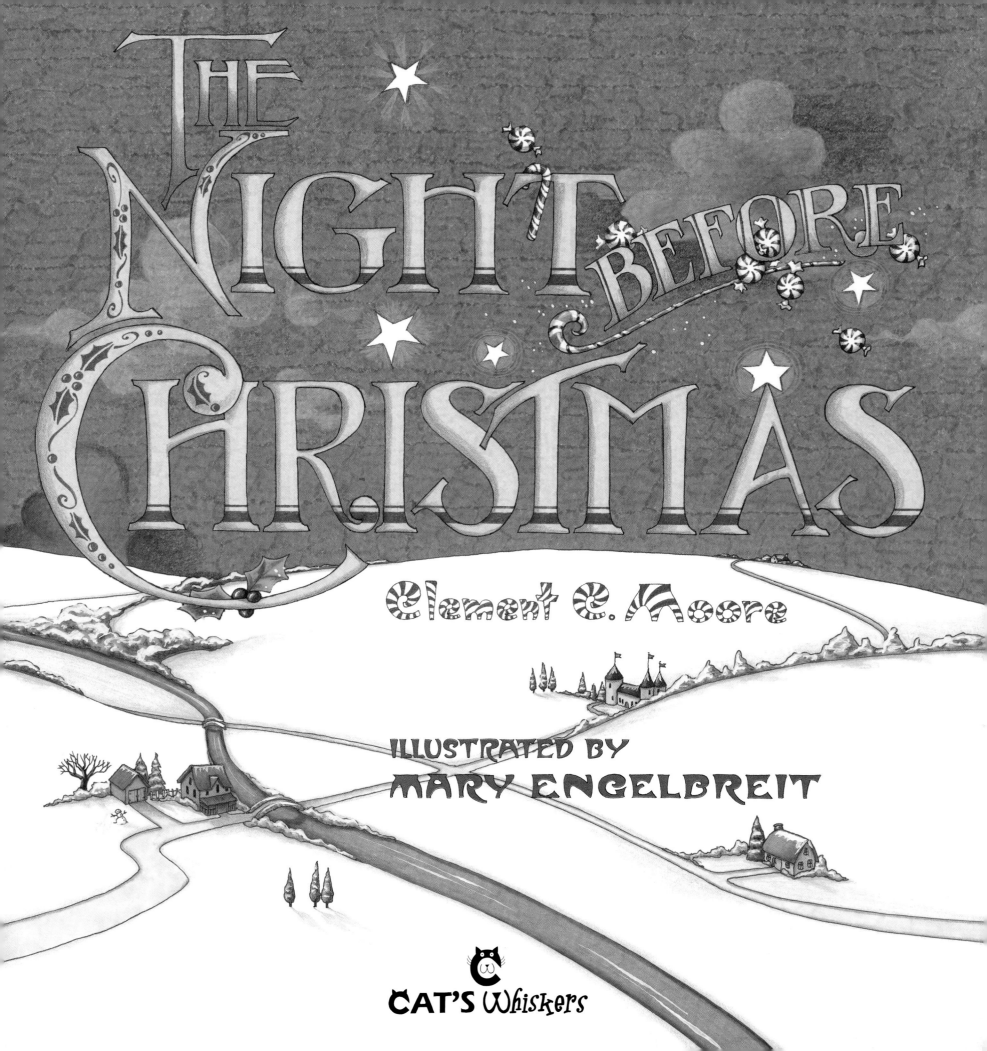

The Night Before Christmas

Clement C. Moore

ILLUSTRATED BY
MARY ENGELBREIT

CAT'S Whiskers

for Will
CHRISTMAS BOY

'Twas the night

before Christmas, when all through the house

Not a creature was stirring, not even a mouse.

The stockings were hung by the chimney with care,

In hopes that St. Nicholas soon would be there.

-FUL' MOUSE WINS
e Sculpture Takes First Place

local mouse, captures the blue
for his cheese sculpture entitled
'E." He's been sculpting all
but this is the first time Art
in an art show. When asked
ed to do with his prize

For Mickey

For SANTA

The children were nestled all snug in their beds,
While visions of sugarplums danced in their heads;
And Mamma in her kerchief and I in my cap
Had just settled down for a long winter's nap.

When out on the lawn there arose such a clatter,
I sprang from my bed to see what was the matter.
Away to the window I flew like a flash,
Tore open the shutters, and threw up the sash.

The moon on the breast of the new-fallen snow,
Gave the lustre of midday to objects below,
When what to my wondering eyes should appear,
But a miniature sleigh, and eight tiny reindeer,

With a little old driver so lively and quick,
I knew in a moment it must be St. Nick.
More rapid than eagles his coursers they came,
And he whistled, and shouted, and called them by name:

"Now, Dasher! Now, Dancer! Now, Prancer and Vixen!
On, Comet! On, Cupid! On, Donder and Blitzen!
To the top of the porch! To the top of the wall!
Now dash away! Dash away! Dash away all!"

As dry leaves that before the wild hurricane fly,
When they meet with an obstacle, mount to the sky;
So up to the housetop the coursers they flew,
With the sleigh full of toys, and St. Nicholas too.

And then, in a twinkling, I heard on the roof
The prancing and pawing of each little hoof.
As I drew in my head and was turning around,
Down the chimney St. Nicholas came with a bound.

He was dressed all in fur, from his head to his foot,
And his clothes were all tarnished with ashes and soot.
A bundle of toys he had flung on his back,
And he looked like a pedlar just opening his pack.

His eyes, how they twinkled! His dimples, how merry!
His cheeks were like roses, his nose like a cherry!
His droll little mouth was drawn up like a bow,
And the beard of his chin was as white as the snow.

The stump of a pipe he held tight in his teeth,
And the smoke, it encircled his head like a wreath;
He had a broad face and a little round belly
That shook, when he laughed, like a bowlful of jelly.

He was chubby and plump, a right jolly old elf,
And I laughed when I saw him, in spite of myself.
A wink of his eye and a twist of his head
Soon gave me to know I had nothing to dread.

He spoke not a word, but went straight to his work,

And filled all the stockings, then turned with a jerk.

And laying his finger aside of his nose,

And giving a nod, up the chimney he rose.

He sprang to his sleigh, to his team gave a whistle,

And away they all flew like the down of a thistle.

But I heard him exclaim, ere he drove out of sight,

This edition 2004
First published in 2003 by
Cat's Whiskers, 96 Leonard Street, London EC2A 4XD
Cat's Whiskers Australia, 45-51 Huntley Street, Alexandria NSW 2015

ISBN 1 903012 73 2

Published by arrangement with HarperCollins Publishers, New York
The Night Before Christmas by Clement C. Moore
Illustrations copyright © 2002 by M. E. Enterprises, Inc